LIBRA

HOROSCOPE

& ASTROLOGY

2025

Mystic Cat

Suite 41906, 3/2237 Gold Coast HWY

Mermaid Beach, Queensland, 4218

Australia

islandauthor@hotmail.com

Contents

Hello there, let me explain why my horoscope books may give different readings for each zodiac sign. The sky is always bustling with astrological activity, and I want to focus on what's most important for each star sign.

Every zodiac sign is unique, and the planets up above affect them differently. When I create horoscopes, I pay extra attention to the most critical astrological events for a specific sign. Some days, there might be lots of stuff happening in the stars, but one thing stands out as the essential factor for a particular zodiac sign.

I also consider which planet rules a sign and its associated element. This in-depth consideration helps me tailor my interpretations to match a sign's characteristics.

Ultimately, my goal is to provide you with unique advice and insights that match the cosmic influences for your sign. By focusing on what makes each sign special, I hope to help you understand yourself better and navigate the energies around you. Embracing your sign's strengths and challenges is the key to making my horoscopes feel uniquely aligned for you.

Cosmic Blessings,

Sia Sands

LIBRA 2025
HOROSCOPE & ASTROLOGY

Four Weeks Per Month

Week 1 – Days 1 - 7

Week 2 – Days 8 - 14

Week 3 – Days 15 - 21

Week 4 – Days 22 – Month-end

LIBRA

LIBRA

Libra Dates: September 23rd to October 22nd

Symbol: Scales

Element: Air

Planet: Venus

House: Seventh

Colors: Pastel blue

LIBRA

Libra is the seventh astrological sign in the zodiac, falling under the Air element. Individuals born under the Libra sign are known for their diplomatic, balanced, and harmonious nature. The symbol of Libra, the scales, represents fairness, justice, and the pursuit of equilibrium.

Libra individuals have a strong sense of justice, social grace, and a natural ability to find common ground. They value harmony and often seek to create a peaceful and balanced environment for themselves and those around them. Ruled by Venus, the planet of love and beauty, Libras appreciate aesthetics and enjoy building harmonious relationships.

Libra is situated in the Seventh House of the zodiac and is associated with partnerships, relationships, and collaboration. This placement emphasizes Libra's inclination toward forming meaningful connections and striving for fairness and equality in interactions.

The pastel blue color is well suited to Libra. This color connection is due to Libra's tranquility, balance, and harmonious relations. This color reflects the calm and diplomatic qualities of Libra individuals.

Libra embodies diplomacy, balance, and harmony. Those born under this sign tend to be skilled at navigating social situations, seeking compromise, and promoting fairness. Their ability to create harmonious connections and their appreciation for beauty make them adept at fostering positive relationships and bringing people together.

The Chinese Zodiac is a system that assigns an animal sign to each year in a 12-year cycle, and each animal is associated with certain personality traits and characteristics.

The Year of the Snake, in particular, holds special significance within Chinese culture and is rich in symbolism.

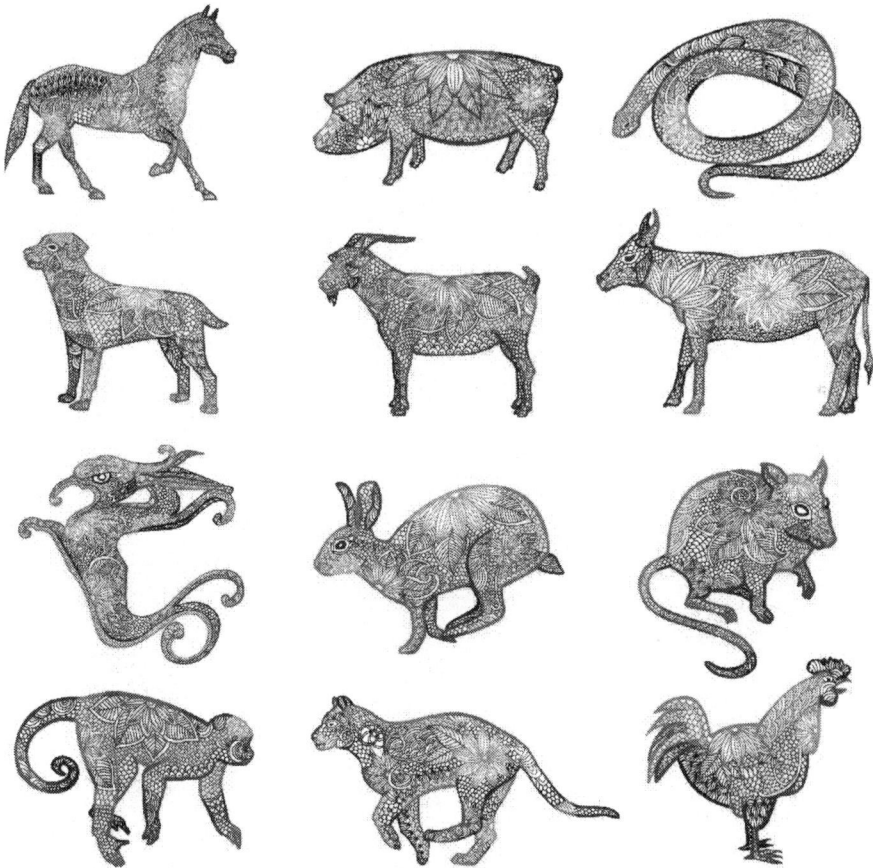

2025

The Chinese Year of the Snake

Libras are known for their harmony-seeking nature, diplomatic skills, and appreciation for beauty. They naturally can create balance in various aspects of life and often prioritize relationships and social interactions. When the Year of the Snake arrives, it introduces a blend of energies that can complement and challenge the Libra personality.

During this year, Libras might find themselves drawn to the Snake's qualities of communication and intuition. Just as snakes use verbal and nonverbal cues to navigate their environment, Libras could enhance their communication skills and connect with others deeply.

The Year of the Snake encourages Libras to explore their diplomatic prowess further. It's a time for them to seek common ground, mediate conflicts, and foster understanding between different perspectives, much like the Snake's ability to navigate diverse terrains.

Libras' appreciation for beauty and aesthetics aligns well with the Snake's sensuality. This year might inspire Libras to create harmonious and aesthetically pleasing environments that reflect their style and balance.

The Year of the Snake could encourage Libras to explore emotional depth in relationships. Just as snakes rely on their senses to understand their surroundings, Libras might find themselves attuned to the feelings and needs of others, cultivating empathy and stronger connections.

While Libras are known for their desire for harmony, the Year of the Snake invites them to explore their inner landscape. It doesn't mean sacrificing diplomacy; instead, it's about combining their social finesse with a deeper understanding of their emotions and motivations.

Ultimately, the Year of the Snake offers Libras an opportunity for personal growth and enhanced relationships. By tapping into the Snake's symbolism of shedding the old and embracing the new, Libras can refine their communication skills, foster deeper connections, and continue creating harmony in their external and internal worlds.

LIBRA 2025

HOROSCOPE & ASTROLOGY

☽ ✦ As the Moon gracefully steps into Capricorn, a shift in your emotional landscape unfolds. Capricorn's energy brings discipline and ambition to the forefront of your emotions, akin to a cosmic CEO taking charge of your feelings. It urges you to set goals and get down to business, fostering a focus on long-term plans and ambitions. Take this time to channel your emotions into productive endeavors, embracing the responsibility that Capricorn brings.

● ✳ Brace yourself because a New Moon is in the mix! This celestial event hands you a fresh canvas and a palette of possibilities. It invites you to set intentions, especially regarding your career and public image. Whether you're aiming for a new job, embarking on a big project, or simply seeking a fresh perspective on your professional life, this is your cosmic reset button.

▨ ⊕ With the Moon gliding into Aquarius, expect an independent and innovative emotional vibe. Aquarius' energy encourages you to break free from the norm and embrace your individuality like a cosmic rebel. It's a time to connect with like-minded souls who share your vision.

❋ Brace yourself for a cosmic serenade as Venus gracefully pirouettes into Pisces. Pisces' energy whispers of deep soul connections, urging you to channel your inner mermaid and let your heart embark on a voyage.

◗ Buckle up, cosmic voyager, for when Mars locks horns with Pluto, the universe orchestrates a grand symphony of intensity and transformation.

☾ As the Moon gracefully waltzes into Pisces, your emotions take on the hues of a dreamy, poetic sonnet. It's a cosmic lullaby, inviting introspection and a connection to ethereal realms.

◉ When the Sun forges a harmonious sextile with Saturn, it's akin to a celestial nod, acknowledging your unwavering dedication and tireless effort. This aspect ushers in stability and an undeniable sense of achievement.

☽ Brace yourself for an electrifying cosmic transition as the Moon enters Aries. This celestial spark ignites your passions and propels you into the forefront of adventure.

Mercury's graceful entrance into Capricorn marks a shift towards more structured and organized thinking. Your mental gears start turning with a practical bent, focusing on long-term goals and solid plans.

The Moon's transition into versatile Gemini turns the spotlight onto communication. Your curiosity becomes insatiable, propelling you into engaging conversations, research, and the pursuit of knowledge.

Later, as the Moon gracefully glides into nurturing Cancer, emotions take center stage. The celestial tide turns toward home and family, creating a deep longing for comfort and heartfelt connections. It's a cosmic embrace, urging you to prioritize self-care and strengthen bonds with loved ones.

Mars forms a harmonious trine with Neptune, infusing your actions with enchantment. You'll find that your energy aligns effortlessly with your intuition and higher creative faculties. The cosmos hands you a mystical paintbrush, allowing you to craft endeavors with inspiration and spiritual insight.

The Sun's harmonious trine with Uranus electrifies your world with innovation and a thirst for change. It's a cosmic wake-up call, encouraging you to break free from routines and embrace new experiences.

The Full Moon, radiant and resplendent, illuminate your path and achievements. It's a moment of cosmic culmination, where you stand in the spotlight, acknowledging your successes and evaluating your aspirations.

As the Moon gracefully enters Leo, your inner performer takes center stage. You'll radiate charisma and confidence, seeking opportunities for self-expression and creativity. The cosmos encourages you to let your unique talents shine and revel in the joy of being yourself.

Venus squares Jupiter, stoking a desire for indulgence and pleasure. While there's nothing wrong with savoring life's finer things, it's essential to maintain balance during this celestial rendezvous. Find joy in life's beautiful moments, cherishing the day.

When the Sun stands in opposition to Mars, it's akin to a celestial clash of willpower and ego. Your desires are intensified, but conflicts may arise due to impulsive actions or aggressive tendencies. This aspect encourages you to balance asserting your needs and avoiding unnecessary confrontations.

As the Moon gracefully enters Virgo, your emotional focus shifts towards practicality and attention to detail. You'll find satisfaction in organization and productivity, making it an excellent time to tackle tasks that require precision and efficiency.

The Sun's harmonious sextile with Neptune adds a touch of enchantment to your life. Your intuition and creativity flourish, and you may find solace in artistic or spiritual pursuits. It's a cosmic embrace of dreams and inspiration.

Venus's conjunction with Saturn brings a sense of commitment and responsibility to your relationships and financial matters. While this aspect may highlight challenges, it also encourages you to build solid foundations in affairs of the heart and money.

Later, as the Moon glides into Libra, the emphasis is on harmony and balance in your emotional world. You'll seek beauty and fairness in your surroundings; a diplomatic and charming touch marks your interactions with others.

Mercury forms harmonious sextiles with Saturn and Venus, amplifying communication skills and mental acuity. You'll find it easier to articulate your thoughts and negotiate effectively, personally and professionally.

The Sun's ingress into Aquarius marks a shift towards intellectual exploration and unconventional thinking. You're drawn to innovation and progressive ideas, making it an exciting period to embrace your uniqueness and socialize with like-minded individuals.

The Sun's conjunction with Pluto brings a profound transformational energy to your life. This cosmic aspect is a time of rebirth and regeneration.

As the Moon moves into Scorpio, your emotions take on an intense and introspective hue. It's a cosmic invitation to dive into the mysteries of your soul.

Mercury's trine with Uranus fuels your mind with brilliant and unconventional ideas. Your thoughts are electric, and you'll find innovative solutions to old problems. Embrace this mental spark and let your creativity flow.

With the Moon's ingress into adventurous Sagittarius, you'll yearn to explore new horizons. Your spirit craves freedom and knowledge, making it an excellent time for travel or expanding your philosophical outlook.

Venus trine Mars ignites your passion and harmony in relationships. Your interactions are filled with affection and desire, deepening emotional connections. It's a cosmic dance of love and craving.

As the Moon moves into practical Capricorn, you'll feel grounded and focused on your ambitions. It's time to roll up your sleeves and tackle responsibilities with determination and discipline.

Mercury's sextile with Neptune adds a touch of magic to your communication. Your words become poetic and intuitive, creating a remarkable period for creative writing and heartfelt conversations.

The Moon's ingress into Aquarius intensifies your need for independence and originality. You'll seek out like-minded individuals who share your perspectives.

Mercury's conjunction with Pluto delves into the depths of your thoughts and brings transformative insights. It's a time to uncover hidden truths and embrace personal empowerment.

The New Moon marks a fresh start and a powerful time for setting intentions. Plant the seeds of your desires and watch them grow.

Uranus turns direct, bringing a shift in the cosmic winds. It's time to embrace change and innovation in a more forward-moving manner.

With the Moon's ingress into compassionate Pisces, your emotions flow like a gentle river. You'll feel empathetic and connected to the world around you.

The Sun's trine with Jupiter radiates optimism and abundance. It's a time of growth and expansion, where opportunities abound, and your spirits are high.

💜 When Venus forms a celestial alliance with Neptune, it's akin to a mesmerizing serenade for your heart and soul. Love and romance take on an enchanting, ethereal quality that encourages you to embrace your inner poet, expressing your affections with artistic flair and profound emotional depth. This cosmic dance invites you to explore the dreamier facets of love, transcending the ordinary and reveling in the extraordinary.

🌙 As the Moon gracefully ushers in the fiery domain of Aries, your emotions are set ablaze with passion and assertiveness.

🌑 Mercury's harmonious trine with Jupiter paints the sky with a vivid intellectual palette. Your communication skills become a tapestry of wisdom and optimism as your mind opens to expansive ideas. Conversations hold the potential for profound insights. It's an auspicious time for learning and sharing knowledge.

🌙 As the Moon waltzes into the sensual territory of Taurus, your emotions find solace in life's simple pleasures and the embrace of stability. This lunar transit encourages savoring the beauty of the present moment.

🐏 With Venus's entrance into fiery Aries, your love life and personal style receive a spirited infusion of boldness and independence. Your affections take on a fearless quality, and you'll have no reservations about taking the initiative in matters of the heart. It's a time to revel in the thrill of romantic pursuits and confidently assert your desires.

⏩ Jupiter's resumption of direct motion signals a dynamic shift towards forward momentum and growth. Projects and plans that may have been temporarily on hold can now progress with renewed vigor as the cosmic winds propel your aspirations and endeavors.

🌙 The Moon's transition into communicative Gemini heightens your social instincts and intellectual curiosity. Your communication skills take center stage, and you'll find great delight in connecting with diverse people, sharing ideas, and engaging in stimulating exchanges.

💜 Finally, Venus's harmonious sextile with Pluto adds depth to your relationships and desires. This passionate and transformative energy encourages you to explore the profound depths of your connections.

As the Moon gracefully transitions into nurturing Cancer, emotions take on a tender and compassionate quality. You'll find solace in the comforts of home and seek to connect with loved ones on an emotional level. This lunar shift encourages you to prioritize self-care and strengthen the bonds of family and close friends.

The Sun's conjunction with Mercury creates a cosmic symphony of communication and self-expression. Your words carry the warmth of the Sun's rays, making it an excellent time to express yourself with clarity and confidence. Your mind is sharp, and you can effectively convey your thoughts and ideas.

Mars forms a harmonious trine with Saturn, infusing your actions with discipline and determination. This cosmic alliance fuels your drive to achieve long-term goals and pursue tasks with unwavering commitment. It's a time of structured progress and systematic efforts.

As the Moon enters bold Leo, your emotions are ignited with confidence and a desire to shine. You'll seek opportunities for self-expression and draw creative endeavors or activities that see you bask in the spotlight.

⚡ The Sun's square with Uranus brings a touch of unpredictability to your life. It's like a cosmic wake-up call, urging you to break free from routine and embrace change. While this can be liberating, be mindful of sudden disruptions.

🌑 The Full Moon shines a celestial spotlight on your achievements and personal goals. It's a time of culmination and reflection, where you can celebrate your accomplishments and reevaluate your aspirations.

🌙 The Moon's transition into meticulous Virgo encourages attention to detail and a focus on practical tasks. You'll find satisfaction in organizing your surroundings and working on projects that require precision.

💜 On Valentine's Day, Mercury gracefully enters empathetic Pisces. This cosmic shift enhances your ability to connect emotionally and intuitively in heart matters. Your conversations become more compassionate and poetic, making it a lovely time for heartfelt expressions of love and affection. It's a perfect alignment for romantic words and gestures.

When the Moon gracefully enters Libra, it's like a gentle breeze sweeping through your emotions. You'll find yourself naturally gravitating toward harmonious interactions and aesthetically pleasing surroundings. This lunar influence encourages you to seek balance and fairness in your relationships, making it an ideal time for diplomacy and compromise. Your desire for peace and equilibrium guides your emotional responses, creating an atmosphere of serenity.

As the Moon transitions into passionate Scorpio, your emotions plunge into introspection. This lunar shift invites you to explore the hidden realms of your psyche, making it a powerful time for transformation. You may find that intuition heightens, allowing you to perceive nuances and unspoken emotions. You'll be drawn to experiences that resonate with your innermost desires.

With the Sun's entrance into compassionate Pisces, you enter a realm of heightened sensitivity and artistic inspiration. Pisces, the sign of the dreamer and the empath, invites you to embrace empathy, imagination, and a deeper connection to the mysteries of existence.

As the Moon transitions into adventurous Sagittarius, a wave of optimism washes over you, and the thirst for exploration is awakened. You'll be naturally drawn to new experiences, seeking philosophical insights and the thrill of the unknown. This lunar phase ignites your wanderlust, encouraging you to break free from routine and embrace the freedom of the open road, whether that's a physical or metaphorical journey. It's when you yearn for physical and mental space and seek expansion in various aspects of your life.

Mercury's square with expansive Jupiter adds an element of enthusiasm to your communication, but it also comes with a caveat. While your ideas may be grand and your words filled with optimism, it's essential to balance visionary thinking and practicality. This aspect encourages you to remain grounded in your plans and avoid overcommitting or making promises that might be challenging to keep. By harnessing the boundless potential of your ideas while staying rooted in reality, you can make the most of this cosmic conversation between Mercury and Jupiter.

As the Moon gracefully transitions into the earthy realm of Capricorn, your emotions take on a practical and goal-oriented tone. It's when you're inclined to set your sights on your ambitions and work steadily toward your objectives. The influence of Capricorn encourages you to take a structured and disciplined approach to your emotional life, emphasizing responsibility and long-term planning. You may find satisfaction in achieving small milestones toward your larger goals.

Mars, the fiery planet of action, turns direct, signaling a decisive shift in cosmic energies. After a period of retrograde motion, you'll feel a surge of vitality and determination. This forward momentum empowers you to pursue your desires with renewed vigor and resolve. It's a time to harness your inner warrior and confidently stride toward your objectives.

The Moon's transition into progressive Aquarius ushers in open-mindedness and a desire for intellectual exploration. You'll be drawn to unconventional ideas and may seek the company of like-minded individuals who share your visionary outlook.

Mercury's conjunction with Saturn signifies a period of structured and deliberate thinking. Your mental faculties are honed for practicality and precision. This cosmic alignment encourages you to approach your communications and thought processes with a sense of responsibility and a keen eye for detail. It's an ideal time for in-depth, systematic work and tackling complex tasks with focus and determination.

The Moon's entry into dreamy Pisces casts a gentle, reflective light on your emotions. It's a phase when you're more attuned to your inner world and may find solace in artistic or spiritual pursuits.

Mercury's sextile with Uranus adds an element of innovation and mental acuity to your thought processes. Your mind is open to exciting and unconventional ideas, and you're inclined to seek intellectual stimulation through unique conversations and experiences. This aspect encourages you to embrace change and view challenges as opportunities for growth.

Venus, the planet of love and beauty, embarks on a period of introspection as it turns retrograde. This celestial event encourages you to reevaluate your relationships and approach to matters of the heart. It's a time to reflect on your values, personal aesthetics, and how you express love and affection. Past connections may resurface, offering an opportunity for healing and growth in love.

Mercury's conjunction with Neptune blurs the lines between reality and imagination, creating an ideal atmosphere for creative and intuitive thinking. Your mind becomes a canvas for artistic and spiritual insights, making it an excellent time for exploring creative projects, meditation, and mystical pursuits. This cosmic connection invites you to listen to your inner voice and express yourself compassionately.

The Sun's square with expansive Jupiter adds a touch of optimism and enthusiasm to your life. While this aspect can bring growth opportunities, balancing grand plans and practical considerations is essential. Your ambitions may soar but remember to remain grounded as you navigate the possibilities that arise.

Mercury's transition into fiery Aries ignites your thoughts with assertive and independent energy. Your communication style becomes more direct and spontaneous, and you'll be unafraid to express your ideas and opinions passionately. It's a cosmic call to speak your mind and passionately pursue your interests.

As the Moon moves into sensual Taurus, you'll find comfort and solace in simple pleasures. Emotionally, security takes precedence, and you may seek to create a harmonious environment that nurtures your senses.

Mercury's sextile with transformative Pluto empowers your words with depth and intensity. You can communicate with insight and impact, delving into the profound aspects of life and human psychology. Conversations may revolve around transformation, healing, and exploring hidden truths.

The Moon's shift into curious Gemini ignites your intellectual curiosity and desire for social interactions. You'll be drawn to diverse conversations and interests, making it an ideal time to connect with others and explore new ideas.

The harmonious trine between the Sun and Mars infuses you with energy and assertiveness. You'll find yourself in a confident and dynamic state, making it an ideal time to tackle challenges and pursue your goals with vigor.

As the Moon gracefully moves into Leo, your emotions take on a regal and expressive quality. It's a time to shine and embrace your inner performer. You'll seek attention, and your creative spark will be ignited, inspiring you to share your talents and passions with the world.

Mercury's conjunction with Venus enhances your communication with charm and grace. Your words are infused with an air of diplomacy and a desire for harmony. This cosmic alignment supports pleasant conversations and the expression of affection in your interactions.

The Moon's transition into meticulous Virgo encourages you to focus on details and get organized. This lunar phase is perfect for decluttering and attending to practical matters.

⬤ The Sun's conjunction with Saturn marks a time of discipline and commitment. Your focus is on long-term goals and responsibilities. This aspect brings stability and a sense of accomplishment as you diligently work towards your objectives.

⬤ The Full Moon illuminates your achievements and long-term goals, offering a moment of celebration and reflection. It's a time to acknowledge your successes and assess your ambitions to ensure they align with your desires.

⚡ The Sun's sextile with Uranus brings a touch of innovation and spontaneity to your life. While it may lead to sudden changes or opportunities, it's also an invitation to embrace your individuality and explore new horizons.

☽ As the Moon continues its journey, entering the harmonious realm of Libra, your emotions are attuned to balance and cooperation. You'll seek harmony in your relationships and surroundings, making it an ideal time for diplomacy and finding compromises.

🔄 Mercury's retrograde journey brings a period of reflection and review to your communication and thought processes. It's as if the cosmic messenger takes a step back, prompting you to revisit and revise your plans and ideas. During this time, please pay close attention to the details and exercise patience regarding your interactions and decision-making.

🌙 As the Moon delves into the enigmatic realm of Scorpio, your emotions take a deep dive into the abyss of feelings and mysteries. There's an inherent urge to uncover hidden truths within yourself and the world around you. During this emotionally charged phase, you may experience heightened intuition and a desire for authenticity in your interactions. Be prepared to embrace the transformative power of vulnerability as you navigate this profound lunar influence.

🌙 When the Moon transitions into adventurous Sagittarius, optimism and curiosity surround you. This lunar phase expands horizons and offers new experiences. You'll be naturally drawn to philosophical insights, learning, and exploring uncharted territory.

☀ The Sun's conjunction with Neptune marks a time of heightened sensitivity and a deep connection to your dreams and intuition. It's like a cosmic invitation to explore creativity, spirituality, and empathy. Your imagination soars, and you may find solace in artistic or spiritual pursuits. Trust your inner guidance during this phase and allow your heart to guide you.

☼ The Sun's transition into Aries heralds the Vernal Equinox, a moment of balance and renewal as we welcome the arrival of spring. Aries energy is dynamic and assertive, encouraging you to embrace new beginnings and take bold steps toward your goals. It's a time of initiation and planting seeds for the future, where your enthusiasm and courage lead the way.

💘 Venus's sextile with Pluto adds depth and intensity to your relationships and desires. This cosmic connection encourages you to explore the depths of your contacts, both in love and personal values. You may experience profound emotional transformations and a stronger desire for authenticity in your interactions. It's a time to embrace the transformative power of love and passion.

As the Moon gracefully transitions into the Earth sign of Capricorn, your emotions become anchored in practicality and responsibility. During this lunar phase, your focus turns toward your long-term goals and commitments. You'll find a sense of satisfaction in taking care of your duties, and your ambition takes center stage, urging you to pursue your aspirations with determination.

The conjunction of the Sun and Venus creates an enchanting aura, casting a radiant spotlight on your relationships and the things you hold dear. This celestial alignment infuses your interactions with a blend of affection and beauty, making it a perfect time to express your feelings and indulge in the finer aspects of life.

When the Sun forms a harmonious sextile with Pluto, your experiences add depth and intensity. This cosmic connection empowers you to explore transformative processes and make meaningful changes. It's a period when you're invited to delve into the core of your desires and emerge with a greater sense of self.

💜 The conjunction of Venus and Neptune amplifies the dreamy and romantic ambiance. Your imagination takes flight, and you draw artistic and spiritual pursuits, finding inspiration in the ethereal and the divine.

🖥 As the Moon strides into Aries, you'll feel energy and assertiveness. This cosmic call to action urges you to take the lead, confidently asserting your desires.

⚫ The arrival of the New Moon signifies a fresh beginning and a moment to set new intentions. During this lunar phase, you are encouraged to plant the seeds of your desires and envision the future you wish to create. It's a time of renewal and a cosmic canvas to paint your aspirations.

🌑 Mercury's ingress into Pisces enhances your intuition and empathy in your communications. Your words take on a more compassionate and poetic tone, making it an ideal period for deep, heartfelt conversations. You'll find a natural ability to connect with others on a profound and soulful level.

As the Moon gracefully transitions into airy Gemini, intellectual curiosity and communicative energy permeate your emotional landscape. You may be eager to engage in lively discussions, exchange ideas, and explore new interests. This lunar phase encourages mental agility and a thirst for knowledge.

Saturn's sextile with Uranus brings a harmonious blend of tradition and innovation to the forefront. This celestial alignment encourages you to find inventive ways to incorporate change and progress into your life while respecting established structures and values. It's a period where you can create a solid foundation for future endeavors.

Mars's sextile with Uranus ignites a fiery combination of assertiveness and adaptability. Your actions are marked by a willingness to break constraints.

Mars's trine with Saturn brings a harmonious fusion of motivation and discipline. You'll find the determination and patience to pursue your ambitions steadfastly. This alignment empowers you to accomplish tasks and overcome obstacles through planning.

⬤ The Sun's sextile with Jupiter bestows a fortunate and expansive energy upon your life. This cosmic connection brings a sense of optimism and opportunity. It's as if the universe offers you a helping hand, enabling you to broaden your horizons and pursue your goals.

💜 Venus's trine with Mars creates an atmosphere of romantic harmony and passion. Your relationships are infused with a delightful blend of affection and desire. This aspect fosters a balance between masculine and feminine energies, enhancing your ability to connect with others on both emotional and physical levels.

♣ Venus's conjunction with Saturn signifies a period of commitment and structure in your relationships. You'll find value in creating enduring bonds built on trust and responsibility. This alignment encourages you to assess your partnerships with maturity and make decisions contributing to long-term stability.

🔄 Mercury's direct motion brings relief from recent communication and logistical challenges. Your thought processes become more straightforward, and misunderstandings are more accessible to resolve.

✦ When Venus forms a sextile with Uranus, it's as if a gentle cosmic breeze sweeps through your relationships and your perception of beauty. This harmonious alignment encourages you to embrace the unexpected and enjoy the unconventional. In matters of the heart, you may be more open to trying new things and connecting with refreshingly different people. This aspect adds a touch of excitement and unpredictability, infusing your life with a dash of spontaneity.

☽ As the Moon gracefully transitions into Virgo, you'll notice a subtle shift in your emotional landscape. Virgo's influence bestows a keen eye for detail and a desire for order. You might find solace in organizing your surroundings or tackling tasks that require precision. This lunar phase is ideal for refining your routines, being more efficient, and addressing practical matters.

💜 Moving into Libra, the Moon encourages you to seek equilibrium and harmony in your emotions and interactions. Libra, represented by the Scales, is the sign of balance, and during this lunar phase, you'll be drawn to fairness and cooperation. It's a time for nurturing relationships as the cosmic diplomat within you shines.

The Full Moon is like a celestial spotlight, illuminating the achievements and culminations in your life. It's a moment of celebration and reflection as you acknowledge the results of your hard work. Emotions run high during a Full Moon, making it an ideal time to release what no longer serves you and embrace the harvest of your intentions. This phase marks a culmination, symbolizing closure and fulfillment.

As Venus turns direct, it's as if the planet of love and beauty has been reawakened. After a period of introspection during its retrograde phase, Venus begins to move forward, renewing your appreciation for all things lovely and romantic. Your relationships regain their sense of progress, and you may find it easier to express affection and connect with others. Your artistic and aesthetic senses are revitalized, encouraging you to explore the world's beauty with a fresh perspective.

The Moon's transition into Scorpio delves deep into intensity and transformation. Your emotional depth and intuition are heightened during this phase, making it an excellent time for introspection, self-discovery, and even delving into complex issues with courage and resilience.

✳ As the Moon dances into adventurous and free-spirited Sagittarius, your emotions take flight. It's like a cosmic invitation to explore new horizons and embrace a more optimistic outlook.

With Mercury's transition into fiery Aries, your thoughts and communication style become more direct and assertive. You're not one to beat around the bush during this period. You speak your mind and take the initiative in your conversations and decision-making.

When Mercury aligns with dreamy Neptune, it's as if your thoughts are touched by a veil of mysticism and intuition. Your imagination soars, and you're more attuned to subtle, spiritual insights. This celestial connection encourages creative thinking and may inspire you to explore artistic or spiritual pursuits.

As Mars enters the fiery sign of Leo, your passions and desires are ignited with enthusiasm. You exude confidence and charisma, making taking the lead in your endeavors easier.

🌙 Mars and Neptune's harmonious connection infuses your actions with compassion and idealism. You're driven by a desire to make a positive impact, and your intuition and a sense of higher purpose may guide your efforts. This alignment encourages exploring spiritual pursuits.

🌷 Easter Sunday brings a sense of renewal and rebirth. It's a time for celebrating new beginnings and the triumph of light over darkness.

💝 When Venus forms a sextile with Uranus, love and relationships take an exciting turn. This cosmic alignment encourages spontaneity and a willingness to embrace unconventional forms of romance. It's a time when you may experience unexpected attractions or exciting social encounters.

💬 Mercury's harmonious connection with transformative Pluto deepens your thinking and communication. You're drawn to explore profound topics and may engage in meaningful conversations. This alignment supports research, introspection, and a desire to uncover hidden truths.

As the Moon gracefully drifts into Pisces, your emotions take on a dreamy and empathetic quality. This lunar phase encourages introspection and a deep connection to your inner world. You may find yourself more attuned to the emotions of others and drawn to artistic and spiritual pursuits.

When the Sun squares Pluto, it's a time of intense transformation and power struggles. This aspect can bring deep-seated issues to the surface, challenging you to confront them and make necessary changes. It's a chance to let go of what no longer serves your growth.

Venus conjunct Saturn represents a serious and committed approach to matters of the heart. It's like a cosmic contract for love and relationships. This aspect encourages you to build lasting and stable partnerships, making it an ideal time for taking your commitments to the next level.

As the Moon moves into Aries, your emotions ignite with fiery passion and assertiveness. This lunar phase encourages independence and self-discovery, making it an excellent time to pursue personal goals.

As the Moon enters Taurus, your emotions become grounded and focused on stability and security. It's when you may find comfort in simple pleasures and a connection to the physical world. This lunar phase encourages you to nurture your resources and build a sense of inner and outer security.

The New Moon marks a fresh start and a time for setting intentions. It's like a cosmic blank canvas where you can plant the seeds of your desires. Use this phase to clarify your goals and start anew.

The Moon's transition into Gemini enhances your communication and curiosity. It's when your mind becomes more agile, and you're eager to learn and share information. Engage in intellectual pursuits and connect with others through conversation.

Venus's ingress into Aries adds a touch of spontaneity and independence to your love life. You may feel more daring in matters of the heart, ready to enthusiastically pursue what you desire. It is a time for taking the initiative in relationships and embracing a sense of adventure.

As the Moon gently glides into Cancer, your emotions seek comfort and security. This lunar transition turns your focus towards home and family, making it an ideal time for nurturing and connecting with loved ones. You may find solace in the familiar and a desire to create a harmonious, cozy environment.

The conjunction of Venus and Neptune creates a dreamy and romantic atmosphere. It's as if your relationships and creative expressions are touched by magic. You'll find beauty in the ethereal and the subtle, making it an excellent time for artistic endeavors, especially those infused with enchantment and imagination.

When Pluto turns retrograde, it signifies a period of inner transformation and reflection. The intensity and power associated with Pluto turn inward, prompting you to reevaluate deep-seated desires and fears. It offers a chance to release what no longer serves your evolution and gain a better understanding of your psychology. This retrograde phase allows you to explore the hidden layers of your psyche, enabling profound personal transformation and empowerment.

Mercury's sextile with Jupiter is like a burst of intellectual inspiration. Your communication is not only expansive but also optimistic. This aspect encourages you to share your ideas and visions with enthusiasm. It's when your mind is open to new possibilities, and you can see the bigger picture.

As the Moon moves into Virgo, your emotions take on a practical and detail-oriented focus. It's when you find satisfaction in organizing and perfecting your surroundings. This lunar phase encourages you to tackle tasks precisely and highlight the finer points.

Venus's sextile with Pluto intensifies your relationships and passions. It's a cosmic connection that deepens emotional bonds and brings a sense of empowerment to your romantic life. You may experience intense desires and profound relationships with others. This aspect encourages you to explore the depths of love and creativity. It's like a passionate, transformative embrace of your desires and connections. You may find yourself drawn to profound, soul-stirring partnerships or artistic pursuits exploring life's mysteries. This aspect encourages you to embrace your inner power.

☀ As the Moon gracefully glides into Libra, your emotions become attuned to balance, harmony, and the pursuit of beauty. This lunar phase inspires you to seek fairness and equilibrium in your relationships and surroundings. You may find yourself drawn to artistic expressions and enjoy diplomatic, peace-seeking interactions with others.

☿ Mercury's entrance into Taurus grounds your communication style in practicality and sensuality. Your words take on a deliberate and steady pace, often infused with a touch of charm and a love for the finer things in life. This transit encourages you to communicate your values and embrace a patient approach to decision-making.

▨ The Moon's journey into intense Scorpio heightens your emotional depth and desire for transformation. It's a time when you're more in tune with the mysteries of life and unafraid to confront hidden truths. This lunar phase encourages you to dive into your passions and explore the depths of your psyche. Your emotional depth and intuition shine brightly.

The Full Moon illuminates the skies with its radiant energy, marking a culmination and a turning point in various aspects of your life. It's a time of revelation and clarity, where the intentions you set during the New Moon reach their peak. This lunar transit is a decisive moment for releasing what no longer serves you and embracing the fullness of your desires.

When Mercury squares Pluto, your thoughts delve into power and transformation. This aspect can bring deep and probing conversations, often touching on subjects others might find uncomfortable. It's a time when you're unafraid to question and dig beneath the surface to uncover hidden truths.

As the Moon shifts into Sagittarius, your emotions take on a more adventurous and freedom-seeking tone. You long for experiences that expand your horizons and seek the truth in all its forms. This lunar phase encourages exploration through travel or intellectual pursuits and a free-spirited approach to life. It's an excellent time for travel, philosophical exploration, and connecting with people from different backgrounds.

As the Moon gracefully moves into Capricorn, your emotions become disciplined and focused on your ambitions. You're ready to climb the mountain of your goals, seeking structure and long-term success. This lunar phase encourages you to take practical steps toward your objectives, whether in your career or personal life.

The Sun's conjunction with Uranus is a dynamic celestial event that sparks innovation and originality. Your individuality shines brightly, and you're open to new ideas and possibilities. This aspect encourages you to embrace change and break free from restrictions, fostering a spirit of rebellion and progress.

Mercury's square with Mars ignites your communication with a fiery and assertive energy. It's a time when discussions can become more heated and impulsive, so it's important to practice patience and diplomacy. This aspect can fuel passionate debates and a strong desire to assert your opinions.

⚫ When the Moon moves into Aquarius, your emotions take on an independent and humanitarian quality. You're more inclined to think about the collective and how you can contribute to causes that matter to you. This lunar phase encourages unique and forward-thinking perspectives.

🕐 The Sun's sextile with Saturn is a harmonious aspect that brings stability and a sense of accomplishment. It's like a cosmic pat on the back for your hard work and dedication. This aspect allows you to build a strong foundation for your long-term goals and take practical steps toward your aspirations.

🌘 As the Moon flows into Pisces, your emotions become dreamy and intuitive, attuned to the mystical and emotional depths of life. This lunar phase encourages introspection, creativity, and a connection to your inner world. You find solace in artistic or spiritual pursuits.

♊ The Sun's entrance into Gemini marks a time of increased curiosity and sociability. You're eager to explore new ideas, connect with others, and engage in lively conversations.

💕 Venus's trine with Mars creates a harmonious dance of love and passion. Your relationships and creative pursuits are infused with a delightful balance of assertiveness and affection. This aspect encourages you to express your desires and pursue your heart's desires with confidence and charm.

☀ The Sun's sextile with Neptune opens the door to imagination and inspiration. It's as if the cosmos invites you to embrace your dreams and tap into your creative potential. This aspect fosters a sense of empathy and a deep connection to your inner world, allowing you to infuse your endeavors with artistic and spiritual energy.

✨ When the Sun forms a trine with Pluto, it's like a cosmic key to transformation and empowerment. You have the opportunity to delve into the depths of your psyche and make profound changes. This aspect encourages you to let go of what no longer serves you and regenerate areas of your life.

🌑 Mercury's conjunction with Uranus sparks inventive thinking and unique ideas. This aspect encourages you to communicate your insights with clarity and flair.

Saturn's ingress into Aries marks a significant shift in the cosmic landscape. The taskmaster planet now emphasizes self-assertion, leadership, and a pioneering spirit. During this transition, you're encouraged to take charge of your ambitions and forge a path to success.

Mercury's move into Gemini brings a lively and communicative energy. You're ready to engage in dynamic conversations, explore a range of interests, and adapt to new information quickly. It is a favorable time for networking and intellectual pursuits.

Mercury's sextile with Saturn offers a blend of practicality and mental discipline. You can effectively organize your thoughts and communicate with precision, making it a favorable aspect for tasks that require attention to detail.

The New Moon signifies a fresh start and an opportunity to set new intentions. It's like a cosmic reset button, allowing you to plant the seeds of your desires and embark on new beginnings. This lunar phase encourages introspection and the formulation of new goals.

✳ When the Moon gracefully enters Virgo, your emotions take on a practical and analytical tone. You become more focused on the details, organization, and efficiency of your daily life. This lunar phase encourages you to pay attention to your health and well-being, making it an ideal time for self-care and tending to tasks that require precision.

✻ As the Moon moves into Libra, your emotions seek balance, harmony, and connection. You're drawn to diplomacy and cooperation in your relationships, making it a favorable time for resolving conflicts and seeking compromise. This lunar phase encourages you to appreciate the beauty in your surroundings and foster harmonious connections with others.

💜 Venus sextile Jupiter forms a delightful aspect that brings a sense of joy and abundance to your relationships and pleasures. You may experience a boost in optimism and opportunities for love and enjoyment. This aspect encourages you to indulge in life's joys and share delightful moments with loved ones.

Mercury sextile Mars ignites your communication and mental processes with enthusiasm and assertiveness. You're ready to express your ideas and thoughts with confidence, making it an excellent time for productive discussions and taking action on your plans. This aspect encourages direct and purposeful communication.

Venus's ingress into Taurus brings sensual and earthy energy to your relationships and values. You're drawn to comfort, beauty, and stability, seeking to enhance your connections through affection and appreciation. This transit encourages you to indulge in life's sensory pleasures and cultivate a more profound sense of security in your partnerships.

As the Moon enters Scorpio, your emotions take on a passionate and intense quality. You may find yourself delving into more profound emotional experiences and seeking transformation. This lunar phase encourages introspection, uncovering hidden truths, and exploring the mysteries of life and the psyche.

☀ Mercury's conjunction with Jupiter marks a time of expansive and optimistic thinking. Your mental horizons widen, and you're drawn to explore new ideas and opportunities. This aspect encourages learning, teaching, and sharing knowledge on a grand scale.

☾ As Mercury moves into Cancer, your thoughts and communication take on a nurturing and empathetic tone. You may find yourself more attuned to the emotions of others and inclined to express your feelings. This transit encourages heartfelt conversations and a focus on matters close to the heart.

✗ Mercury square Saturn may temporarily introduce challenges in communication. It's essential to be patient and precise in your interactions, as this aspect can bring obstacles and delays. While it may slow progress, it also offers an opportunity to refine your plans and ideas.

♐ When the Moon gracefully enters Sagittarius, your emotions become adventurous and freedom-loving. You're eager to explore horizons, both mentally and physically. This lunar phase encourages you to expand your worldview and embrace spontaneity.

⚱ Venus square Pluto brings intensity and transformation to your relationships and values. While this aspect may bring about power struggles or conflicts, it also offers an opportunity to dive deep into emotional matters. It's a time for examining your desires and understanding the dynamics of your closest connections.

🏠 Jupiter's ingress into Cancer signifies a shift in the cosmic landscape. This expansive planet now emphasizes family, home, and emotional well-being. It encourages growth and abundance in your domestic life, making it a favorable time for nurturing your roots and strengthening your connections with loved ones.

🌑 The Full Moon is a culmination of energy and emotions, illuminating what has been brewing beneath the surface. It's a time for revelations, completions, and a release of what no longer serves you. This lunar phase encourages reflection and the harvest of your efforts.

💞 Mercury's sextile with Venus adds a touch of harmony and charm to your conversations. You'll find it easier to express affection and appreciation for others.

⚡ Mars square Uranus creates a cosmic storm of unpredictability and restlessness. It's like a lightning bolt shaking up your actions and decisions. This aspect encourages you to embrace change and be cautious of impulsive behavior. Expect the unexpected and exercise caution during this dynamic transit.

⚖ Jupiter square Saturn brings a tug of war between expansion and restriction. It's as if a cosmic referee is making sure you balance your ambitions with practical limitations. This aspect encourages you to be realistic about your goals and responsibilities while still reaching for your dreams.

🌙 As the Moon gracefully moves into Pisces, your emotions take on a dreamy and empathetic quality. It's like a cosmic lullaby, encouraging introspection and a connection to the mystical realms.

🔺 Mars's ingress into Virgo ignites your desire to take action with precision and practicality. It's a time for attention to detail and a focus on the nitty-gritty. This transit encourages you to roll up your sleeves and work diligently towards your goals, making every effort count.

As the Moon enters Aries, your emotions gain a burst of energy and enthusiasm. It's like a cosmic alarm clock, waking your inner go-getter. This lunar phase encourages you to initiate new projects, embrace your independence, and fearlessly pursue your desires.

Jupiter square Neptune creates a cosmic fog around your ambitions and ideals. It's a bit like trying to navigate through a misty forest. This aspect encourages you to remain open to inspiration while keeping your expectations in check. While dreaming big is essential, grounding your visions in reality is equally important.

As the Moon moves into Taurus, your emotions take on a steady and sensual quality.

The Sun's ingress into Cancer marks the June Solstice, a time when the Northern Hemisphere experiences the longest day, and the Southern Hemisphere welcomes the winter solstice. It's a turning point in the year, emphasizing themes of home, family, and emotional connections. Cancer's nurturing energy encourages you to focus on your inner sanctuary and loved ones during this season.

Sun square Saturn presents a challenge to your ambitions and self-expression. It's like a cosmic reality check, where responsibilities and limitations may temporarily overshadow your creative endeavors. This aspect encourages you to develop patience, discipline, and a strong work ethic.

Sun square Neptune creates a subtle tension between your ego and your dreams. It's like a cosmic fog that blurs your sense of self and direction. This aspect invites you to examine your boundaries and discern between healthy idealism and unrealistic illusions.

Sun conjunct Jupiter is a burst of optimism and opportunity. It's like a cosmic green light, signaling a period of expansion, growth, and positivity. This aspect encourages you to embrace life's abundance and possibilities with open arms.

The New Moon marks a fresh beginning and a blank cosmic canvas. It's a time for setting intentions and planting seeds for future growth. This lunar phase encourages reflection and the initiation of new projects or goals.

Mercury's ingress into Leo brings a more confident and expressive tone to your communication style. You'll be more inclined to speak from the heart, share your opinions with flair, and engage in creative forms of expression.

Mercury trine Saturn offers a harmonious blend of discipline and mental acuity. It's like a cosmic scholar's alignment, supporting concentration, practical thinking, and a structured approach to your tasks.

Mercury trine Neptune creates a gentle flow of inspiration and intuition in your thoughts and communication. It's like a cosmic storyteller's gift, enhancing your empathy, creativity, and spiritual insights.

Mercury opposed Pluto introduces intensity and depth to your mental processes. It's like a cosmic detective's challenge, urging you to dig beneath the surface and explore hidden truths. This aspect encourages transformation through honest and profound conversations.

As the Moon enters Scorpio, your emotions take a cosmic plunge into the depths of your feelings and innermost desires. This lunar phase encourages self-reflection, transformation, and a willingness to confront emotional issues head-on.

Venus's conjunction with Uranus creates an electrifying and unpredictable influence on your relationships and desires. It's like a cosmic spark that ignites sudden attractions and the urge for freedom in matters of the heart. This aspect encourages you to embrace change and break free from routine.

Venus's move into Gemini brings light and breezy energy to your love life and social interactions. It's like a cosmic shift from deep to casual, making connections and conversations more playful and versatile. This transit encourages you to explore diverse interests and keep things interesting.

Neptune's retrograde motion turns your focus inward, like a cosmic introspective journey. During this period, you'll reassess your dreams, ideals, and the boundaries of your imagination.

⚹ Venus sextile Saturn creates a stabilizing influence in your relationships and finances. It's like a cosmic assurance of commitment and responsibility. This aspect encourages you to build solid and lasting connections, as well as to manage your resources wisely.

☾ Venus sextile Neptune adds a touch of romance and sensitivity to your interactions. It's like a cosmic wave of empathy and artistic inspiration. This aspect encourages you to express your feelings through creative pursuits and to foster compassion in your relationships.

⚡ Uranus's ingress into Gemini marks an era of intellectual curiosity and innovation. It's like a cosmic switch that turns on your mental creativity and a thirst for knowledge. This transit encourages you to embrace change in your thought patterns and communication styles.

☀ Venus trine Pluto deepens your connections and intensifies your passions. It's like a cosmic force that strengthens the bonds in your relationships and encourages transformation. This aspect brings a magnetic allure and a desire for emotional experiences.

As the Moon gracefully moves into Capricorn, you'll find your emotional landscape adopting a more grounded tone. During this lunar transit, you're encouraged to evaluate your long-term goals and the structures that underpin your life, seeking a harmonious blend between your emotional needs and your worldly responsibilities. This phase prompts a contemplative approach to your feelings as you embrace a strong sense of determination in the pursuit of your objectives.

The Full Moon is a celestial spectacle that symbolizes the peak of emotional energy and a release of what no longer serves you. It's like a cosmic floodlight illuminating your achievements and emotions. This lunar climax encourages you to reflect on your journey, both personal and collective, and to acknowledge your accomplishments with gratitude. It's also a time to let go of emotional baggage and make room for fresh intentions and desires that align with your evolving self.

As the Moon ventures into the intellectual and unconventional realm of Aquarius, a sense of individualism and innovative thinking pervades your emotional landscape.

⏳ Saturn turning retrograde heralds a period of deep introspection and review regarding your responsibilities and long-term aspirations. It's like a cosmic mentor asking you to reevaluate the foundations of your life. During this time, you're encouraged to assess the structures you've built, ensuring they align with your authentic desires and ambitions. This retrograde motion prompts a thorough examination of your commitments, fostering a sense of wisdom and understanding as you refine your life's path.

🌙 With the Moon's entrance into Pisces, your emotions take on a dreamy and empathetic quality. It's as though a cosmic artist washes your inner world with a palette of ethereal colors. This lunar phase encourages introspection, a heightened awareness of your innermost feelings, and a deep connection to the mystical and imaginative realms. Your empathy and compassion for others are amplified during this time, making it an ideal period for exploring your spirituality and the nuances of your emotional landscape. Through reflection and introspection, you'll navigate this cosmic tapestry with wisdom and grace.

As the Moon gracefully enters the fiery realm of Aries, you'll feel a surge of passionate energy infusing your emotions. It's like a cosmic call to action, beckoning you to embrace your inner warrior. During this lunar phase, your feelings are intense and impulsive, encouraging you to take the lead and charge into new adventures. Aries' influence inspires you to assert your desires with unbridled enthusiasm, making it an excellent time for starting new projects and pursuing your passions.

When Mercury, the planet of communication and thought, turns retrograde, it marks a significant celestial event. It's as if the cosmic messenger asks you to pause and engage in a deep conversation with your inner self. During this introspective period, you'll find yourself reflecting on past experiences, reevaluating your thoughts and beliefs, and reconsidering how you communicate with others. This cosmic phase encourages self-awareness and revisiting unresolved matters.

☽ Transitioning into Taurus, the Moon brings a soothing sense of stability and grounding to your emotional landscape. During this lunar phase, you'll be drawn to life's simple pleasures - indulging in delicious food, enjoying the beauty of nature, and relishing sensory experiences. Taurus invites you to nurture your senses and find emotional security in the material realm.

❤ When Mercury forms a harmonious sextile with Venus, it's as if your thoughts and emotions engage in a delightful dance. This celestial connection fosters sweet and meaningful communication. Your conversations become imbued with affection and understanding, making it an ideal time for expressing your love and appreciation for those close to your heart. During this period, relationships are harmonious, and you'll find it easier to convey your sentiments.

☽ The Moon's transition into Gemini ushers in a curious and communicative atmosphere for your emotions. It's like a cosmic storyteller awakens within you, urging you to share your thoughts and feelings with the world. This lunar phase stimulates intellectual curiosity and encourages you to engage in lively conversations.

⚡ When the Sun forms a sextile with Uranus, it's like a cosmic jolt of electricity invigorating your spirit. This aspect encourages innovation, freedom, and unexpected opportunities. You'll feel more open to change and eager to break free from routines. It's a period of exploration where you can embrace your individuality and tap into your inventive side.

⌛ When the Sun forms a trine with Saturn, it's like a cosmic pat on the back for your hard work and dedication. This harmonious aspect brings stability, discipline, and a sense of accomplishment. It's an ideal time for long-term planning, setting goals, and making steady progress in your endeavors. You'll find it easier to stay organized, meet your responsibilities, and build a strong foundation for your future.

🌙 The Sun's trine with Neptune introduces a touch of magic and inspiration to your life. Neptune is the planet of dreams and illusions, and this aspect encourages you to explore your creative and spiritual side. It's a period when your intuition and empathy are heightened, making it easier to connect with others on a deep emotional level.

● The New Moon represents a fresh start and a blank canvas. It's a time for setting intentions and planting seeds for the future. This lunar phase encourages you to reflect on your goals, dreams, and desires and to initiate new beginnings. Embrace this period to set clear intentions, make wishes, and embark on a journey of self-discovery.

● When the Sun opposes Pluto, it's like a cosmic power struggle. Pluto represents transformation and profound change, and this aspect can bring intense confrontations and challenges to the surface. You may find yourself facing power struggles or uncovering hidden truths. It's essential to navigate these energies with awareness and a willingness to let go of what no longer serves you, embracing transformation and rebirth.

○ When the Sun conjuncts Mercury, your thoughts and communication become aligned and illuminated. This aspect sharpens your intellect and encourages open communication. You'll find it easier to express your ideas, make decisions, and convey your thoughts. It's a time for productive discussions and mental clarity.

♥ When Venus squares Saturn, the cosmic stage is set for a dramatic tango between love and responsibility. It's as if you're torn between the desire for romantic connections and the weight of your obligations. This aspect can bring forth feelings of restriction and limitations within your relationships. You might find yourself questioning the longevity and solidity of your emotional bonds. It's important to tread carefully, striving to strike a balance between your emotional desires and the commitments you've made.

◐ Venus square Neptune adds a touch of dreamy confusion to the matters of the heart. It's as if you're navigating through the ethereal mist of illusions and fantasies. This aspect has the potential to lead to misunderstandings in your relationships. You might find yourself idealizing someone or envisioning a love that doesn't necessarily align with reality. During this time, it's crucial to trust your intuition and approach your emotional connections with a discerning eye. While Neptune's influence can create romantic, almost otherworldly experiences, it's essential to ensure that your emotions are grounded in truth and authenticity.

♐ As the Moon journeys into Sagittarius, your emotions take on an adventurous and free-spirited quality. It's like a cosmic call to embark on a thrilling expedition of the heart. This lunar placement encourages you to embrace a broader perspective, seek out opportunities for growth, and satisfy your curiosity through new experiences. Your emotional landscape becomes one of optimism and a hunger for knowledge.

♑ When the Moon transitions into Capricorn, a more grounded and pragmatic emotional energy begins to dominate. It's as if you're beckoned to focus on your responsibilities, long-term goals, and the practical aspects of life. During this lunar phase, you may find fulfillment in tackling tasks, meeting commitments, and making progress in your professional life.

♎ Mars's ingress into Libra introduces an energy of balance and diplomacy to your actions. This cosmic shift encourages you to approach conflicts with grace and cooperation rather than confrontation. Your efforts are focused on creating and maintaining equilibrium in your life, and your actions are aimed at fostering peace and understanding.

When Mars forms a trine with Uranus, you're in for a dynamic and electrifying energy boost. You'll find it easier to take risks and pursue your goals with an unconventional and assertive approach. This cosmic alignment fuels your passion and drive, making it an excellent time to embark on new, exciting ventures.

Mars's opposition to Saturn introduces a clash between your assertive, impulsive side and your need for structure and discipline. This aspect may bring frustration and obstacles, making it challenging to move forward with your plans. However, it also offers an opportunity to reassess your strategies, refine your goals, and build a solid foundation for your ambitions.

The Full Moon is a culmination of energies and emotions, where the Sun in one sign opposes the Moon in the opposite sign. This phase illuminates your relationships and brings any imbalances to the forefront. It's a time of heightened emotions and a chance to gain clarity on your needs and desires. Embrace the insights offered by this Full Moon to find equilibrium in your personal and professional connections.

As Mars opposes Neptune, a sense of confusion and haziness descends upon your actions and desires. It's like trying to navigate through a foggy landscape. This aspect may bring moments of doubt, making it challenging to assert yourself with clarity. It's crucial to stay grounded, as unrealistic goals or deceptive influences can lead you astray. Take time to clarify your intentions before taking any significant actions.

When Mars forms a trine with Pluto, you're granted a surge of transformative and empowering energy. It's as if you've tapped into a deep well of determination and intensity. This aspect encourages you to dig beneath the surface and address hidden desires and issues. Your willpower is formidable, making it an ideal time to make significant changes and pursue your goals with unwavering determination.

Mercury's direct motion signals a shift from introspection to forward momentum. Any communication and technology glitches experienced during its retrograde phase begin to resolve. It is a favorable time to make decisions, sign contracts, and move projects forward with clarity and confidence.

⚡ When Mercury and Mars form a harmonious sextile, it's akin to a celestial collaboration that elevates your mental and communicative abilities. During this period, your thoughts are sharp, and your words are infused with determination. It's as if you've been given a cosmic boost in the realms of cognitive agility and assertiveness. This alignment is ideal for tackling tasks that require strategic thinking and proactive communication. Whether you're diving into problem-solving, embarking on essential conversations, or simply mapping out your plans, you'll find that your words are not only precise but also carry a dynamic energy.

🌙 As the Moon gracefully transitions through the versatile sign of Gemini, your curiosity takes the lead. It's like a refreshing breeze for your intellectual pursuits. Your mind becomes a sponge, eager to soak up new information and explore fresh ideas. This lunar influence encourages you to engage in stimulating discussions, dive into books or educational resources, and fully embrace the diversity of knowledge that surrounds you.

✦ The reappearance of Mercury's sextile to Mars is akin to a cosmic encore. It's a reminder from the universe that your mental acumen and assertive communication are still in the spotlight. This aspect not only enhances your problem-solving skills but also empowers you to convey your ideas with conviction. It's a period when you can cut through mental fog with ease and make a strong impact in your interactions.

☽ When the Moon moves into Cancer, emotions step into the limelight. This lunar placement creates a tender and nurturing atmosphere. You might find yourself more attuned to your feelings and the emotions of those around you. It's a time when the comforting embrace of home and family becomes particularly significant. Connecting with loved ones and finding solace in the familiar are highlighted during this lunar phase.

☀ TheMoon's journey through spirited Leo brings a touch of the dramatic and a desire for self-expression. It's a time when you're drawn to creative endeavors and perhaps a bit of theatrics. This lunar influence encourages you to embrace your inner artist, share your unique talents, and shine in the metaphorical spotlight.

❀ As the Sun enters Virgo, you'll likely feel a shift in your focus and energy. Virgo's influence encourages attention to detail, practicality, and a desire for order. It's a time when you may find satisfaction in tackling tasks that require precision and organization. This transit can spark an appetite for self-improvement and a strong work ethic.

☻ The arrival of the New Moon marks the beginning of a fresh lunar cycle, offering opportunities for setting new intentions and embarking on a path of personal growth. It's a time for reflection, goal setting, and planting the seeds of your aspirations. With the New Moon's energy, you can channel your intentions and dreams into actionable plans.

⚡ When the Sun forms a square with Uranus, expect a burst of unpredictability and innovation. Uranus is the planet of change and originality, and this aspect can infuse your life with a touch of excitement and unconventional thinking. Be open to unexpected opportunities, and don't be afraid to break free from routines.

💜 Venus' harmonious trine to Saturn adds stability and commitment to your relationships and endeavors. This aspect supports lasting connections and can help you build a solid foundation in matters of the heart.

⚙ Venus' sextile to Uranus can introduce a dash of excitement into your love life. You may be more open to trying new things and embracing change, particularly in your relationships. This aspect encourages you to be adventurous and experiment.

🌙 Venus' trine to Neptune carries dreamy and romantic energy. It enhances your emotional sensitivity and can lead to profound, soulful connections with others. It's a time when love and artistry intertwine, inspiring your imagination.

🌙 Uranus' sextile to Neptune is a harmonious aspect that combines the innovative energy of Uranus with the dreamy, intuitive qualities of Neptune. This alignment can inspire creative and spiritual growth, making it a time to explore new horizons and expand your awareness.

As Saturn eases into the watery realm of Pisces, it's like dipping your toes into the ocean of emotions. This transition encourages a deep dive into your inner world. You might feel drawn to explore your dreams, spirituality, and the intricacies of your feelings. It's a time for empathizing with others and nurturing your compassionate side. Saturn in Pisces invites introspection, where you can reassess your long-term goals through the lens of your heart.

When Mercury takes up residence in Virgo, your mental faculties sharpen, akin to fine-tuning a delicate instrument. You'll excel in tasks requiring precision and organization. This period supports your analytical thinking and problem-solving abilities. It's a green light for tidying up your life, and health and wellness will be high on your agenda.

A Mercury square to Uranus electrifies your mental landscape. It's like a sudden lightning strike of inspiration. Your thoughts become more original and unconventional, opening the door to new ideas and perspectives. But be mindful of potential restlessness – your mind may race with innovation.

☝ With Mars squaring Jupiter, a gust of adventurous energy sweeps in. You're ready to expand your horizons and take on challenges with vigor. This aspect fuels your ambitions, making you feel unstoppable. However, be careful not to bite off more than you can chew. Balancing enthusiasm with realistic planning will lead to your most tremendous success.

🔄 As Uranus turns retrograde, it's akin to a journey inward through the corridors of your psyche. You'll retrace the steps of the changes and innovations you've encountered lately. This phase is about integrating these insights, seeking a deeper understanding, and finding your unique path to personal liberation. Self-discovery is the name of the game.

😊 The Full Moon shines a light on your accomplishments, marking a time to reap the rewards of your recent efforts. Reflect on the goals and intentions set during the New Moon. Emotions might run high, so use this phase for self-awareness and introspection. Celebrate your progress and adjust your course as needed. Embrace this opportunity for growth and self-discovery as you navigate the cosmic currents.

The Moon's ingress into Aries ignites a fiery passion within you. You'll feel an upsurge of enthusiasm, courage, and eagerness to take the lead. It's a time when your emotions are unapologetically bold, making it the perfect moment to initiate new projects or champion your unique individuality. Aries' assertive energy encourages you to step out of your comfort zone and embrace fresh experiences with open arms.

As the Moon gracefully glides into Taurus, a sense of groundedness and practicality envelops your emotions. You'll seek comfort, security, and the simple joys of life. This lunar phase is an excellent time to focus on matters of finance and indulge in the sensory pleasures of the physical world.

The Sun's harmonious sextile with Jupiter paints a canvas of optimism and opportunity in your life. This cosmic connection inspires you to broaden your horizons and embrace new adventures. Your confidence soars, making it an ideal period to set ambitious goals and work towards realizing your dreams. This alignment encourages you to see the bigger picture and believe in the abundance of possibilities.

☽ With the Moon gracing Gemini, your curiosity knows no bounds. This lunar influence encourages you to engage in lively conversations, learn something new, and connect with others. It's a time when your mind is agile, and your thirst for knowledge is insatiable. Embrace the spirit of exploration and intellectual growth.

✳ Mercury's sextile with Jupiter enhances your communication skills and expands your intellectual horizons. Under this influence, your ability to express ideas with clarity and enthusiasm is heightened. It's an excellent period for planning, studying, and sharing your thoughts with a broader audience. This alignment fuels your optimism and encourages a positive outlook on life.

⬡ The Sun's conjunction with Mercury deepens the alignment between your thoughts and self-expression. Your mental clarity and articulation are at their peak during this phase. It's a time when your ideas and communication effortlessly harmonize, making it ideal for essential conversations, decision-making, and pursuing your intellectual interests. Your words carry weight, and your mind is a beacon of illumination.

♥ The harmonious sextile between Venus and Mars creates an enchanting atmosphere where love and desire blend seamlessly. This celestial dance sets the stage for romantic connections and heightened passions. You'll find that relationships flow with grace and affection.

✳ Mercury's ingress into diplomatic Libra ushers in a period of balanced and cooperative communication. Under this cosmic influence, you'll be inclined to seek harmony in your interactions, making it an ideal time for resolving conflicts and nurturing mutual understanding.

🌑 On the flip side, Mercury's opposition with Neptune introduces a dreamy and somewhat bewildering quality to your thought processes. This aspect encourages creativity but also warrants caution regarding misunderstandings. Verify details and maintain clarity in your conversations.

🚀 Mercury's trine with both Uranus and Pluto unleashes a wave of intellectual brilliance and transformative insights. This cosmic alignment propels your mental agility and adaptability, enabling you to break free from conventional thinking and embrace innovative ideas.

✿ Venus' entrance into pragmatic Virgo encourages a more analytical and systematic approach to matters of the heart. You'll discover pleasure in attending to the finer details of your relationships, fostering a sense of appreciation for the little things.

⚡ Yet, the square between Venus and Uranus injects an element of unpredictability into your love life. Be prepared for unexpected changes and unconventional romantic interests. This aspect encourages you to embrace the thrill of the unknown.

☼ The Sun's opposition with responsible Saturn may present challenges related to self-expression and personal authority. You might encounter obstacles that demand patience, determination, and a strategic approach to overcome.

● With the arrival of the New Moon, you're granted a fresh beginning and a chance to set new intentions. This cosmic moment marks an opportunity for self-discovery and personal growth. Plant the seeds of your aspirations and be open to the exciting possibilities on the horizon.

◉ With the fiery ingress of Mars into Scorpio, your life gains a remarkable intensity. Passion and determination fuel your every move. The cosmic energy invites you to dig deep, confronting challenges head-on with resilience and unwavering focus. This phase empowers you to pursue your goals with newfound vigor, making it a suitable time for transformation and self-discovery.

✿ The September Equinox marks a shift in the cosmic balance, signaling a transition from one season to another. This celestial event encourages you to find equilibrium in your life, mirroring nature's ability to adapt to changing seasons. It's a time to reflect on your aspirations and priorities, bringing a sense of alignment with the natural world's cyclical rhythm.

♎ As the radiant Sun moves into harmonious Libra, the cosmos spotlights your relationships. You're inclined to seek balance, harmony, and fairness in your interactions, both personal and professional. This period prompts you to address any imbalances and foster a sense of equilibrium in your connections.

⚡ The Sun's trines with Uranus and Pluto usher in a period of transformation and innovation. You'll find yourself more open to change, new experiences, and fresh ideas. Personal growth takes center stage, enhancing your adaptability and resilience.

☽ As the Moon moves into Scorpio, your emotions take on a more intense and reflective quality. It's a time for deep self-reflection and understanding the driving forces behind your actions and feelings.

♨ However, the square between Mars and Pluto intensifies power dynamics and potential conflicts. Diplomacy is vital to successfully navigating this aspect. Avoid provoking confrontations and seek common ground to resolve any challenges.

🌑 The Moon's transition into adventurous Sagittarius brings a sense of expansion and open-mindedness. Emotionally, you're drawn to explore new horizons, both intellectually and experientially. Your wanderlust is ignited during this lunar phase.

As the Moon gracefully dances into Aquarius, you'll likely find a renewed sense of freedom and independence. This celestial shift encourages you to break away from the ordinary and explore uncharted territory. Your mind opens up to innovative and unconventional ideas, making it an ideal time to engage in intellectual pursuits or contribute to humanitarian causes. Feel the winds of change and embrace the spirit of individuality as you navigate this cosmic influence.

The square aspect between Mercury and Jupiter brings an interesting cosmic clash. While you may be overflowing with enthusiasm and optimism, there's a need to balance this with a practical approach. The devil is often in the details, and this aspect challenges you to find a happy medium between your grand visions and the nitty-gritty specifics of your projects. Remember that, with the right balance, your expansive thinking can meet real-world success.

As the Moon moves into fiery Aries, your energy surges, and you're ready for action. Aries' dynamic and assertive influence can help you pursue personal goals and passions with vigor. It's a time to seize the moment.

Mercury's transition into Scorpio adds a layer of depth and intensity to your thinking. During this period, you'll find yourself inclined to investigate matters more thoroughly, uncovering hidden truths and diving beneath the surface of issues. It is a phase that encourages deep introspection and a desire to get to the bottom of complex and mysterious topics.

The Full Moon, with its radiant glow, illuminates your path. It signifies a time of culmination and realization. Reflect on the intentions you set during the New Moon and see how they've developed. It is a powerful opportunity to release what no longer serves you and move forward with clarity and purpose. The Full Moon's light can guide you to achieving goals and intentions.

However, the square between Mercury and Pluto adds an intense flavor to your communication and thought processes. While you may be exceptionally determined and focused, it's essential to be mindful of becoming too fixated on ideas or getting entangled in power struggles. Keep your lines of communication open and maintain a flexible approach to avoid becoming overly obsessed with specific outcomes.

🌙 As the Moon gracefully waltzes into Taurus, a celestial calm settles over you, urging a connection with the earthly pleasures of life. Sink into the luxurious embrace of sensual experiences, savoring the simple joys that touch your senses. It's a cosmic invitation to appreciate the beauty that surrounds you, grounding your emotions in the serenity of the material world.

✿ The harmonious sextile between Venus and expansive Jupiter paints your interactions with strokes of warmth and grace. Social connections bloom under this cosmic alignment, fostering generosity and shared enjoyment. Take delight in the finer things, and let the spirit of abundance color your relationships with an air of joy.

🌑 Venus, now gracefully pirouetting through Libra, engages in a cosmic tango with stern Saturn. This dance introduces a subtle tension into matters of love and aesthetics, emphasizing the delicate balance between desires and practical considerations. Patience and diplomatic finesse become your cosmic allies. It brings depth to your experiences of love and creativity.

🌙 🖤 ✨

💜 Venus, adorned in Libra's elegance, brings a touch of refinement to your interactions. However, an opposition with dreamy Neptune adds a poetic layer of ambiguity. Navigate matters of the heart with caution, aiming for clarity amidst the romantic reverie.

🔄 Pluto's direct motion signals a cosmic shift, urging you to embrace transformation and shed lingering shadows. This period is a call to profound inner growth, encouraging you to release what no longer aligns with your highest good.

✳ The Moon's entrance into Leo brings a radiant and theatrical energy to the cosmic stage. Express your authentic self with confidence, basking in the creative spotlight that encourages self-assurance.

🌙 Venus, in a harmonious trine with the innovative Uranus, introduces a sprinkle of excitement into your love life and creative pursuits. Embrace spontaneity and remain open to unconventional expressions of affection.

🐚 Venus's trine with Pluto deepens the hues of passion and intensity in your connections. This cosmic alignment invites transformative experiences.

🌙 The Moon gracefully enters Virgo, ushering in a phase where attention to detail and practicality take center stage. You may find a sense of fulfillment in attending to the finer points of life, focusing on organization, and pursuing activities that contribute to your overall well-being.

✦ A cosmic tension arises as the Sun squares Jupiter, signaling a period where the desire for expansion and growth may clash with the need for moderation. It's essential to find a balance between optimism and practicality, ensuring that your aspirations are grounded in a realistic approach.

🌙 Transitioning into Libra, the Moon invites you to seek harmony and balance in your relationships and surroundings. This cosmic shift encourages a diplomatic and cooperative approach, fostering connections that are characterized by fairness and mutual understanding.

○ Mercury's conjunction with assertive Mars sparks a surge in communicative energy. Your words carry the vigor of Mars, and conversations may have an extra edge of intensity.

● A New Moon graces the celestial canvas, marking the beginning of a lunar cycle ripe with potential for new beginnings. It is a cosmic blank slate, inviting you to set intentions, embark on fresh ventures, and embrace a spirit of renewal. Take time to reflect on your desires and aspirations, allowing the energy of the New Moon to guide you forward. Consider your goals, aspirations, and the areas of your life where you seek fresh beginnings. Harness the energy of this New Moon to set intentions that align with your authentic self.

◪ As the Moon moves into Scorpio, emotions deepen, and a desire for introspection emerges. This lunar phase encourages you to delve into the mysteries of your inner world, embracing transformative experiences that promote personal growth and healing.

These cosmic movements guide you through a journey of meticulousness, a balance between optimism and practicality, harmonious connections, assertive communication, and the initiation of new beginnings. Each phase holds unique energies, inviting you to navigate your path with intention and authenticity.

🌙 🌙 ✦

● The Sun's square with transformative Pluto intensifies the cosmic energies, creating a potent atmosphere of power dynamics and metamorphosis. This celestial alignment challenges you to confront and release aspects of your life that no longer serve your growth. Embrace the metamorphic process, trusting that from the ashes, new beginnings emerge.

🌟 Mercury, the messenger of the cosmos, forms harmonious trines first with expansive Jupiter and then with structured Saturn. These aspects enhance your communication skills, blending optimism with practicality. Engage in meaningful conversations, share your ideas with confidence, and seek a balanced approach to your thought processes.

🚀 The harmonious dance between assertive Mars and expansive Jupiter brings a surge of dynamic energy and motivation. This cosmic collaboration propels you forward, providing the courage and enthusiasm to pursue your goals with vigor. Leverage this momentum to take bold strides toward your aspirations.

♐ Mercury's ingress into adventurous Sagittarius amplifies the quest for knowledge and truth. Your mind expands as you seek a broader perspective on life's mysteries. Embrace a spirit of exploration, indulge in philosophical discussions, and let your curiosity lead you to new horizons.

⚙ Mars' trine with disciplined Saturn adds a layer of structure to the cosmic energies. This alignment empowers you with the endurance and strategic thinking needed to overcome challenges. Approach your endeavors with a methodical mindset, and you'll find that disciplined actions yield fruitful results.

⚡ Mercury's opposition with unpredictable Uranus introduces an element of surprise and innovation to your mental landscape. Embrace the unexpected, stay open to new ideas, and allow spontaneity to infuse excitement into your thought processes.

🔄 Mercury's sextile with transformative Pluto deepens the cosmic narrative, inviting you to delve into profound insights and embrace the power of regeneration. Engage in meaningful conversations, as they are transformative.

The Moon's fiery ingress into Aries sets a dynamic tone, infusing you with a burst of energy and a desire for action. Embrace this spirited momentum to initiate new projects or embark on exciting adventures.

Venus squares Jupiter, creating a cosmic tension between the planet of love and beauty and the expansive energy of Jupiter. This alignment may bring about a clash between desires for pleasure and the need for moderation. Be mindful of indulgence and seek a balance between enjoyment and responsibility in matters of the heart.

Mars forms a harmonious trine with Neptune, blending the assertive drive of Mars with the dreamy and imaginative influence of Neptune. This cosmic collaboration inspires creative initiatives fueled by intuition. Channel your energy into artistic pursuits or projects that align with your higher aspirations.

Mars' ingress into Sagittarius marks a shift in the cosmic landscape, infusing your actions with a sense of adventure and enthusiasm. This transit encourages you to pursue your goal, embracing the spirit of exploration.

The Full Moon illuminates the skies, casting its glow on the culmination of endeavors and highlighting areas of your life that require balance. Take stock of your achievements and release what no longer serves you to make room for new growth.

Mars sextile Pluto intensifies the transformative potential of your actions. This cosmic alliance empowers you to delve deep into your pursuits, fostering profound changes and regeneration. Embrace the potency of focused and strategic efforts.

The Moon's ingress into Gemini invites a shift in your emotional focus, encouraging intellectual curiosity and social interactions. Engage in meaningful conversations and allow your mind to explore various perspectives.

Venus' ingress into Scorpio deepens the emotional currents in matters of love and relationships. Dive into the depths of your connections, exploring the complexities and intensities that make partnerships truly transformative. In this celestial journey, Venus in Scorpio intensifies emotional connections.

◎ Get ready for a cosmic shift as Uranus, the planet of innovation and sudden change, makes its entrance into Taurus. This celestial event sets the stage for a profound transformation in the realms of stability and security. Brace yourself for a period of radical shifts, urging you to embrace flexibility and openness to groundbreaking ideas that challenge the status quo. This transit encourages a departure from the ordinary and an exploration of unconventional paths that promise exciting breakthroughs.

💔 Venus square Pluto intensifies the cosmic drama, delving deep into the intricate landscape of your relationships. This powerful and transformative aspect brings forth profound realizations and challenges, urging you to confront and overcome obstacles. It's a cosmic invitation to undergo a metamorphosis in matters of the heart, breaking through old patterns and paving the way for renewed connection.

🌙 As the Moon gracefully glides into Cancer, the cosmic energy takes a nurturing turn. It's a celestial embrace encouraging you to find solace in the comforts of home, fostering an understanding of your emotional needs.

🔄 Mercury embarks on its retrograde journey, prompting a period of introspection and review. This cosmic realignment encourages you to revisit old projects, relationships, and unresolved issues. Exercise caution in communication, expecting delays and providing ample space for revisiting past matters with newfound clarity.

🔍 Jupiter, the expansive planet, takes a reflective pause as it turns retrograde. This cosmic realignment prompts you to reassess personal beliefs, philosophies, and growth goals. Use this period for inner exploration, refining your path, and gaining a deeper understanding of your spiritual journey.

🤝 Mercury's conjunction with Mars amps up communication and mental agility. Leverage this dynamic energy to express your thoughts assertively. However, be mindful of potential conflicts arising from impulsive words, and channel this energy into productive endeavors. This dynamic alignment empowers you to express your thoughts assertively and tackle tasks with precision.

The harmonious trine between the Sun and Jupiter is like a cosmic blessing, infusing your days with optimism, growth, and a sense of abundance. You're on the receiving end of positive energy, encouraging you to expand your horizons, pursue opportunities, and embrace the joy of the present moment.

Sun's trine with Saturn adds a touch of stability to your endeavors. This cosmic alliance provides a solid foundation for your ambitions, allowing you to build with discipline and lasting success. It's a time for responsible actions and reaping the rewards of your hard work.

Mercury, the planet of communication, forms a sextile with transformative Pluto. Your thoughts and words carry a profound impact, and your ability to delve into the depths of matters is heightened. This aspect encourages deep conversations, research, and the uncovering of hidden truths.

Mercury's entrance into Scorpio intensifies your mental focus. You're drawn towards uncovering secrets and delving into the mysteries of life.

● The New Moon heralds a fresh start, offering a blank canvas for new intentions and beginnings. Set your goals, plant the seeds of your desires, and trust in the cosmic support for your aspirations.

◐ Sun's conjunction with Mercury in Sagittarius brings a burst of expressive energy. Your communication style becomes more adventurous and optimistic. It's a time to share your ideas, engage in lively conversations, and embrace a broader perspective.

◎ Uranus's sextile with Neptune weaves an ethereal thread through the cosmic fabric. This alignment encourages you to explore the intersection of innovation and spirituality. Embrace inspiration from unexpected sources, and let your creativity flow freely.

🖋 Sun's opposition to Uranus introduces an element of surprise and unpredictability. Be open to sudden shifts and innovations in your life. Embrace change, even if it deviates from your usual path.

🐏 Sun's trine with Neptune brings a wave of inspiration and creativity. It is an excellent time for artistic pursuits, spiritual practices, and compassionate actions.

Communication gains a touch of grounded wisdom as Mercury forms a harmonious trine with Saturn. Your thoughts and words are infused with practicality and a long-term perspective. Use this cosmic connection to build solid foundations for your ideas and projects.

A celestial conversation between Mercury and Jupiter enhances your mental prowess and expands your intellectual horizons. Your mind is open to grand ideas, and you may find yourself drawn to learning or teaching on a broader scale. This alignment fosters positive thinking and the ability to see the bigger picture. Take advantage of this cosmic synergy to explore new concepts and communicate with optimism and enthusiasm.

The Sun forms a harmonious sextile with Pluto, infusing your journey with transformative energy. This celestial aspect empowers you to tap into your inner strength and make positive changes in your life. You have the resilience to overcome challenges and the power to influence your circumstances. Embrace this cosmic support to delve into personal growth and embrace the potential for positive transformation.

💜 The harmonious trine between Venus and Jupiter creates an atmosphere of abundance and joy in matters of love and pleasure. This celestial dance encourages you to indulge in the finer things in life and to expand your capacity for love and enjoyment. It's a time to celebrate relationships, appreciate beauty, and bask in the positivity that surrounds you.

🔲 The cosmic harmony between Venus and Saturn brings stability and commitment to your relationships and creative endeavors. This alignment emphasizes the importance of building lasting foundations in matters of the heart and artistic pursuits. Your connections deepen, and your creative projects gain structure and longevity under this celestial influence.

🔄 The cosmic messenger, Mercury, resumes its direct motion, lifting the fog of retrograde energies. Communication flows more smoothly, and any delays or misunderstandings begin to resolve. Use this time to move forward with plans, make decisions, and express your thoughts with increased clarity.

♥ A celestial dance unfolds as Venus forms a harmonious sextile with Pluto, infusing the atmosphere with magnetic allure and transformative energies. Relationships and desires take center stage, offering a profound opportunity for deep connection and profound change. Under this cosmic alignment, passions may intensify, and a magnetic pull towards the profound and the mysterious weaves its enchanting tapestry in matters of the heart.

☽ The Moon, now donning the versatile cloak of Gemini, ushers in a breeze of intellectual curiosity and communicative flair. Thoughts flutter like butterflies, and emotions are expressed with a playful dance of words. Gemini's influence encourages adaptability and a thirst for knowledge. Embrace the lightness of this lunar phase, and let the mind soar on the wings of curiosity.

● The cosmos orchestrates a celestial spectacle as the Moon reaches its full brilliance, casting a luminous glow upon the night sky. This Full Moon brings a culmination of energies, illuminating the seeds planted during the preceding lunar cycle.

🌙 The Moon, finding solace in the nurturing waters of Cancer, invokes a tender embrace of emotions and a deep connection to the hearth of the soul. Sensitivity becomes a guiding force, encouraging a retreat into the comfort of home and family. Cancer's influence fosters a compassionate atmosphere, inviting individuals to cherish and protect that which holds emotional significance. Allow the lunar tide to cradle the heart in its gentle ebb and flow.

✳ A celestial dance unfolds as Mercury forms a harmonious trine with Neptune, weaving an ethereal tapestry of imagination and intuition. This cosmic alignment invites a time of heightened creativity, spiritual insights, and a subtle yet profound connection to the mystical realms. Let the boundaries between reality and fantasy blur as the mind explores the poetic depths.

🌙 The Moon takes center stage as it gracefully enters the regal realms of Leo, bringing a burst of theatrical energy and a radiant display of emotions. Leo's influence encourages a flair for self-expression, urging individuals to shine like cosmic performers.

◖ Mars, the warrior planet, squares off against Saturn, the taskmaster, creating a celestial battlefield where the clash between desire and responsibility takes center stage. This cosmic tension calls for a strategic approach to your goals, blending passion with discipline to overcome challenges on your path.

☽ The Moon gracefully enters Virgo's meticulous domain, inviting you to embark on an emotional cleanup. Detail-oriented and practical, this lunar transit encourages you to organize your feelings, promoting a sense of order within your inner world.

◪ Neptune, the dreamy planet, turns direct, lifting the veil on illusions and casting a clarifying light on your visions. With Neptune's fog dissipating, your dreams and inspirations gain sharper focus, allowing you to navigate with renewed insight.

↯ Mercury, the messenger, engages in a celestial tug-of-war with Uranus, sparking intellectual fireworks. Expect the unexpected in your thoughts and communications as Uranus challenges the status quo, inspiring innovative solutions and unique perspectives.

Mercury, in a harmonious trine with Neptune, weaves a tapestry of enchanting words. Your communication takes on a poetic and empathetic quality, fostering deep connections and understanding.

Mercury embarks on a Sagittarian adventure, expanding the horizons of your mind. Embrace the spirit of exploration, allowing your thoughts to roam freely and discover new intellectual territories.

The Moon's ingress into Libra brings a celestial breeze of harmony to your emotional landscape. Relationships take center stage, urging you to seek fairness, cooperation, and aesthetic balance in your interactions.

Mercury's sextile with Pluto adds depth and intensity to your communications. Dive fearlessly into profound conversations, unearthing hidden truths and fostering transformation through the power of words.

Mars, in a challenging square with Neptune, asks you to navigate the murky waters of ambition. Be mindful of illusions and ensure that your actions align with reality.

🌙 The Moon gracefully slides into intense Scorpio, inviting you to explore the depths of your emotions. This cosmic transit encourages introspection and a willingness to delve into the shadows of your soul. Embrace the transformative power of vulnerability.

♐ As Mars, the cosmic warrior, enters structured Capricorn, the battlefield shifts to the realm of ambitions and achievements. This celestial combination fuels your drive for success, urging you to approach your goals with resilience and strategic precision.

☀ The Sun squares off against stern Saturn, creating a cosmic tension between your vitality and the demands of responsibility. This celestial clash calls for a balance between ambition and practicality. Consider this a checkpoint to assess the solidity of your foundations.

🌑 The New Moon graces the sky, marking the beginning of a lunar cycle. This moment is a potent time for planting seeds of intention and setting fresh goals. Embrace the darkness of the night as a canvas for your dreams to unfold.

🌙 The Moon transitions into disciplined Capricorn, urging you to approach your emotions with a sense of responsibility.

⚫ The mysterious Black Moon slips into philosophical Sagittarius, casting a veil of introspection over your beliefs and ideals. Dive deep into the caverns of your convictions, reassessing what holds in the light of your evolving wisdom.

⚪ The Sun squares off against elusive Neptune, creating a cosmic dance between reality and illusion. Be cautious of illusions and deceptive influences. This celestial configuration encourages you to ground your aspirations in practicality.

💔 Venus engages in a celestial duel with Saturn, challenging the harmony in your relationships. This cosmic tension calls for a reassessment of commitments and a commitment to building solid foundations in matters of the heart.

❉ The December Solstice marks a celestial turning point, welcoming a shift in the balance between light and darkness.

♥ As Venus twirls in a celestial dance with Neptune, a captivating yet potentially intricate energy surrounds matters of the heart. The lines between reality and illusion may blur, emphasizing the importance of careful judgment in navigating your relationships. Be cautious about overly idealizing situations or individuals, and strive for transparency in your emotional connections.

♣ Venus elegantly transitions into the organized realm of Capricorn, introducing a sense of structure and responsibility to your expressions of love and admiration for beauty. During this phase, practical considerations may play a significant role in your romantic pursuits, encouraging you to establish solid foundations. Small, considerate gestures of love can prove incredibly impactful in this period.

☾ The Moon drifts into the dreamy waters of Pisces, inviting you to explore the poetic landscapes of emotion and intuition. This cosmic alignment enhances your sensitivity and compassion, creating an ideal moment for artistic endeavors, meditation, or introspective journeys to connect with your inner self.

🌙 Experience a shift in the lunar atmosphere as the Moon boldly enters Aries, bringing forth a surge of initiative and a strong desire for action. Feel the dynamic force propelling you forward, encouraging you to confront challenges head-on and assert your individuality in various aspects of life.

♠ Continuing on its celestial journey, the Moon transitions into the grounded realms of Taurus. Embrace the pleasures of the material world, taking time to savor and find solace in the stability of your surroundings. Allow yourself to indulge in sensory experiences that bring comfort and joy.

☐ Mercury finds itself in a celestial dance with Saturn, creating a cosmic tension between communication and structure. Navigate this alignment with thoughtful and deliberate expression while being mindful of potential challenges or limitations in conveying your ideas.

▨ Watch as the Moon gracefully pirouettes into the inquisitive realms of Gemini, igniting intellectual curiosity and enhancing communication skills. Explore new ideas and revel in the adaptability that it brings.

NOTES

112

NOTES

Astrology, Tarot & Horoscope Books.

Mystic Cat

Printed in Great Britain
by Amazon